SAVANNAH

classic

SEAFOOD

SAVANNAH classic SEAFOOD

Recipes from Favorite Restaurants

JANICE SHAY

Photography by Deborah Whitlaw Llewellyn

PELICAN PUBLISHING COMPANY
Gretna 2010

Edited by Kerry Shay and Sara LaVere

The word "Pelican" and the depiction of a pelican are trademarks
of Pelican Publishing Company, Inc., and are registered in
the U.S. Patent and Trademark Office.

ISBN-13: 978-1-58980-744-0

Layout based on a design by Kit Wohl

Printed in Singapore

Published by Pelican Publishing Company, Inc.
1000 Burmaster, Gretna, Louisiana 70053

To my talented stepson, Kerry,
without whose editing
and cooking skills this book
would not exist; and to
my husband, Patrick, who
inspires me daily to reach
for the stars.

Contents

Chapter 1   CRAB

Crab Stew	Crystal Beer Parlor	15
Deviled Crabs	Russo's Seafood	16
Corn and Crab Chowder	Firefly Cafe	18
Savannah Crab Cakes	Savor... Savannah	20
Shrimp and Crab Au Gratin	Johnny Harris Restaurant	23
Seafood Cheesecake	Sundae Café	24
She Crab Soup	Olde Pink House	26

Chapter 2   FISH

Fried Grouper Fingers	Tubby's Tank House	31
Sweet Potato-Crusted Grouper with Peach Chutney	Sundae Café	32
Whole Red Snapper with Roasted Vegetables	Olympia Café	35
Parmesan Crusted Grouper with Jumbo Lump Crabmeat	Pearl's Saltwater Grill	36
Salmon Cakes with Cilantro Cream Sauce	Soho South Café	39
Crab Stuffed Flounder	Uncle Bubba's Oyster House	40
Pan-Roasted Black Grouper	Chef Joe Randall	43
Pan-Seared Red Snapper	Driftaway Cafe	44

Chapter 3   OYSTERS

Confederates on Horseback	Mrs. Wilkes' Boardinghouse Restaurant	49
Oyster Dressing	Martha Giddens Nesbit	50
Oyster Stew	Cafe 37	53

Oyster Po' Boy	Cafe 37	55
Cornmeal Fried Oysters	Pearl's Saltwater Grill	56
Bloody Mary Oyster Shooters	Savor... Savannah	58
Fried Oyster Caesar Salad	Olde Pink House	60
Scalloped Oysters	Martha Giddens Nesbit	62

Chapter 4　　SHRIMP

Watermelon and Wild Georgia Shrimp Salad	Kayak Kafé	66
Capt'n Crab's Low Country Boil	The Crab Shack	68
Pickled Shrimp	Susan Mason Catering	71
Caribbean-Spiced Boiled Shrimp	North Beach Grill	72
Seafood Casserole	Mrs. Wilkes' Boardinghouse Restaurant	75
Shrimp and Onion Quiche	17Hundred90	76
Crab-Stuffed Shrimp	The Lady & Son's	79
Shrimp, Greens, & Grits	Belford's	80
Shrimp & Grits	Kasey's Gourmet Grille	83
Boiled Shrimp	Tubby's Tank House	84

Chapter 5　　SCALLOPS

Spring Greens and Pan-Seared Scallops with Citrus Vinaigrette	Chef Joe Randall	88
Scallop Ceviche	Chatham Club	91
Margarita Grilled Scallops	Sundae Café	92

INDEX

INDEX	94

INTRODUCTION

"A loaf of bread, the Walrus said,
Is what we chiefly need:
Pepper and vinegar besides
Are very good indeed—
Now if you're ready, Oysters, dear,
We can begin to feed!"

LEWIS CARROLL,
Alice Through the Looking-Glass

Like Lewis Carroll's "Walrus," I'm not a patient diner—I'm a persnickety one. I like my seafood fresh and local, and not surprisingly, I'm never disappointed with what Savannah's restaurants offer. The success of any seafood recipe is directly dependent upon the quality of the catch, and I'm happy to report that the lag time from boat to table is blissfully short in Savannah.

Coastal towns have a symbiotic relationship with the sea that colors the history and life of the city. From the sky, Savannah and the surrounding Low Country looks like an intricate silvery spiderweb of creeks, rivers, marshes, and streams that feed into the Atlantic Ocean. Twice daily, seven-foot tides sweep the intracoastal waterways, revealing abundant oyster beds. It is a rich marine environment that yields a variety of fresh seafood, and Savannahians have been delighting in our coastal cuisine since the area was first settled in 1733.

The city's history, as well as its cuisine, is bound to the sea and the peculiarities of southeastern geography. The influence of the many peoples—English, Spanish, French, Irish, Gullah—who have helped populate the Low Country added color and spice to our traditional dishes.

The city looks to the sea for its revenue as well as our bounty of seafood. Today Savannah is a major commercial port—the proximity of the city of Savannah to the Atlantic Ocean has long aided the city in becoming a thriving port. By 1773, Savannah had already established itself as a significant commercial port on the South Atlantic coast, exporting 2 million pounds of deer hides annually. By the time of the Civil War, vast exports of Georgia cotton made Savannah the vital reason for Sherman's March to the Sea.

Savannah's elegant historic district is the home of many of the great restaurants and caterers who have contributed their recipes to this cookbook, and the visitors who come to the city are blessed with a wealth

INTRODUCTION

of fabulous dining choices. In fact, a recurring problem I had compiling this book was choosing which traditional recipes to include, because so many good ones are available. I daresay there isn't a restaurant or cafe here that doesn't include crabcakes, Low Country boil, shrimp and grits, or a seafood stew on their menu. There is such a fierce competition among local chefs to serve the best crabcakes that I could easily have included ten or more equally mouthwatering versions!

Tybee Island is Savannah's beach community, located a mere twenty minutes from downtown, and I have included recipes from three great restaurants there. Tybee is a whimsical and "fish-centric" beach, and a good starting point for visitors to get in touch with our Low Country marine environment. It is approached through marshes teeming with oysters and crab, and as you drive over Lazaretto Creek Bridge to get to the island, you might catch a glimpse of the colorful parade of shrimpers returning with their daily haul. Serious fishermen head to the piers early mornings to try their luck. Artistically painted and decorated turtle sculptures are found everywhere around the island; an eclectic roadside market features fish sculptures made from found objects; a popular shop, Seaside Sisters, offers beach signs, furniture, and ship-worthy items to take home; and dockside bars and marinas serve a vast menu of local seafood, blackened, baked, boiled or fried, but always fresh and good.

Enjoy and eat hearty, 'mates!

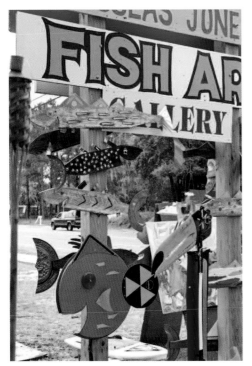

A view of Savannah's historic downtown River Street, and the ferry that takes visitors across the river. Container ships on their way to the port frequently pass by, to the enjoyment of crowds on River Street.

CRAB

Don't ever try to tell a native Savannahian that crab cakes taste better in another part of the country. I've heard that Maryland's version of this delightful dish is excellent, but you'd have a hard time proving it. You see, Savannah blue crab meat is the basic ingredient for the perfect crab cake, and we'll never be convinced otherwise, so how in the world could the crabcakes in Maryland taste any better? You'll need to taste a Savannah blue crab for yourself and decide if this is just convoluted Southern logic, or if we are really onto something.

I'd never seen a crab trap when I moved to Savannah two decades ago. Now, I look for them at every dockside restaurant and marina that I visit. The colorful wire boxes are a promise that you're about to dine on something incredibly fresh and tasty. Because blue crab meat is so versatile and abundant, it has inspired a savory slew of traditional dishes, including soups, stews, au gratin, and deviled crabs.

CRYSTAL BEER PARLOR
CRAB STEW

SERVES 8

2 tablespoons salted butter
8 tablespoons all-purpose flour
1/2 cup yellow onion, minced
1 quart whole milk
1 quart heavy cream
2 teaspoons salt
1/2 teaspoon white pepper
2 tablespoons Worcestershire sauce
1/4 teaspoon Tabasco Sauce
2 tablespoons lemon juice
1 1/2 pounds picked crab meat, backfin or
   claw
1/2 cup dry sherry (optional)

Melt butter over medium heat in a large pot. Add minced onion and cook, stirring occasionally until onions are translucent. Add flour and cook, stirring until flour is blended in well. Add milk and heavy cream gradually, stirring constantly until smooth. Add seasonings and stir until well blended. Just before serving, add lemon juice and crabmeat (and sherry, if using). Stir until heated through, garnish with lemon wedge and a sprig of parsley, and serve.

Brothers John and Phillip Nichols are looking to continue a long tradition of lively spirits and great food in Savannah. In 2009, the two re-opened Savannah's second oldest bar and restaurant, the famous Crystal Beer Parlor.

The restaurant first opened in 1933 and is rumored to have been a speakeasy and a place where men came to play cards during Prohibition. It's no surprise then that it was one of the first places in the country to serve alcohol after the laws were repealed. Since then, the bar and restaurant have been a gathering place for generations of Savannahians.

Walking into the Parlor feels like stepping into a bygone era with the old wooden booths and historic photographs covering the walls. It is a great place to enjoy a drink and reminisce about all the good times and great meals that have been shared there. Although the burgers are no longer 30 cents, they are rumored to be some of the best in town, along with the local favorites, creamy crab stew and oyster "poor-boy" sandwiches.

RUSSO'S SEAFOOD DEVILED CRABS

SERVES 8

2 pounds claw crabmeat
½ cup onions, finely chopped
¼ cup bell pepper, finely chopped
¼ cup celery, finely chopped
½ stick butter
2 eggs, beaten
8 real crab shells
1 1/2 sleeves of Ritz Crackers
1/4 cup ketchup
Dash cayenne pepper
2 tablespoons mustard
2 tablespoons Worcestershire sauce
2 tablespoons Johnny Harris BBQ sauce, or
    your favorite brand
1 tablespoon salt
1/2 tablespoon pepper

Saute celery, onions, and bell peppers in butter until tender. Place mixture in a large mixing bowl and beat in the eggs. Add all other ingredients and mix thoroughly. Fill 8 crab shells with the mixture and bake in a 350 degrees F oven until brown on top.

Charles Russo Jr. is something of a local celebrity in Savannah. A few years ago, "Charlie"—as many affectionately call him—tried to open a restaurant in midtown Savannah to accompany his well-known retail seafood business. Although the city refused his request to re-zone the property, Charlie opened the restaurant anyway. To the dismay of many locals, the city found out and the restaurant had to shut its doors. Soon after, many Savannahians were seen with "Free Charlie Russo" stickers on their bumpers!

Russo's Seafood is considered the best place in the city to get the freshest catch of shrimp, fish, and crabs. The family-run wholesale and retail seafood distributor has served the community for over 60 years and has helped preserve the tradition of wild-caught, fresh seafood in Savannah. It's also a great place to get all the tartar sauce and fixin's you will need to have a Savannah-style feast.

About 50 years ago, Charlie's mother started mixing up the deviled crabs and freezing them to sell at the seafood store. She started making just a half dozen each day, but when the word got out about how good her deviled crabs were, sales skyrocketed and today Russo's deviled crabs are still a top-selling item at their store.

FIREFLY CAFE
CORN AND CRAB CHOWDER

SERVES 8

1 pound claw crabmeat
8 tablespoons unsalted butter
2 cups red onion, finely diced
1 cup flour
2 quarts chicken stock
1 cup carrots, finely diced
2 1/4 pounds red potatoes, finely diced
2 cups Half & Half
4 cups fresh corn, off the cob
1/2 tablespoon black pepper
2 tablespoons salt
2 teaspoons Tabasco

Downtown's Troupe Square is the home of a favorite Savannah eatery, Firefly Cafe. The area was the home of a string of unsuccessful restaurants until 2002 when Sharon Stinogel and Lisa Carr partnered to open Firefly Cafe. Since then, the casual corner cafe has thrived on it's comfortable atmosphere, great food, and welcoming staff. Recently bought by Liam and Darcy O' Connor, the new owners plan to build on their restaurant's reputation.

Firefly has one of the city's best selections of wholesome vegetarian cuisine, and they also offer comfort food—delicious classics such as Dressed Up Mac N' Cheese and Peach Bread Pudding. The outdoor tables that line Habersham Street are a great place to enjoy a meal outside and are part of the reason why the cafe was named Savannah's "Best Place for Saturday/Sunday Brunch" by Connect Savannah in 2006. The inside dining area often features the work of local artists and the outdoor tables have a great view of Troupe Square and some of the prettiest restored townhouses in the historic district.

Melt the butter in a heavy pot, add the red onions, and saute until soft, about 5 minutes.

Add the flour and cook an additional 5 minutes, stirring constantly to prevent burning. Add the chicken stock one quart at a time, stirring well after each addition. Allow the soup to thicken before adding the next quart of stock.

Add the carrots and potatoes and cook until tender, about 20 minutes. Add the corn and Half & Half, and simmer for another 10 minutes. Season before serving with Tabasco, salt and pepper.

If the crab meat has been refrigerated, heat it in a microwave or pan tile warm. Put 2 ounces of crab meat in the bottom of each bowl, ladle the hot soup over the top, and serve.

SAVOR... SAVANNAH
SAVANNAH CRAB CAKES

SERVES 8

2 pounds jumbo lump crabmeat

2 cups mayonnaise

4 to 6 each egg whites

2 cups Panko (Japanese bread crumbs
   or saltines, crumbled)

1/2 cup white bread crumbs

1/2 cup fresh lemon juice

1/2 teaspoon white pepper

1/8 teaspoon cayenne pepper

1/2 cup vegetable oil

Salt to taste

FRIED CAPER FLOWERS
1/2 cup nonpareil capers

1 cup olive oil

REMOULADE SAUCE

1/2 cup whole grain mustard

1/2 cup prepared horseradish

1/4 cup green onion, finely chopped

1/2 cup capers, drained

1/2 cup gherkins, finely chopped

2 tablespoons sugar

2 1/2 tablespoons paprika

1 1/2 teaspoons Worcestershire

2 teaspoons granulated garlic

1 cup mayonnaise

24 cherry tomatoes

Savor... Savannah's staff is a highly trained team that really knows how to put on a culinary show for a range of occasions, whether it is a classy black-tie dinner, an entertainment event, or a business convention. Their food is consistently excellent, whether they are cooking for a party of twenty or two hundred.

As the exclusive caterer of the Savannah International Trade and Convention Center, this group gets lots of chances to show off the local food of the Low Country. Savor... Savannah often caters at some of the most sophisticated venus in town, including the cafe at the Jepson Center For The Arts and affairs at the Owens-Thomas House.

Executive Chef Jamie Parks prepares dishes with fresh ingredients and an emphasis on the natural flavors that they offer. Many of their events showcase the region's flavors with the all the flair of a fine-dining experience, so that guests can get a taste of the best of what the city has to offer.

Pick the shells from the crabmeat, making sure not to break up the larger lumps. Refrigerate until needed.

Combine the mayonnaise, egg whites, Panko, bread crumbs, lemon juice, parsley, and peppers. Salt to taste. Mix until well blended, then gently fold in the crabmeat, keeping the lumps whole.

Form the crabmeat mixture into 16 (2 ½ to 3-inch) round cakes. Pack gently and place the cakes on a baking sheet about 2 inches apart, cover with plastic wrap, and refrigerate for 2 to 4 hours.

To make the remoulade sauce, combine the mustard, horseradish, green onion, capers, gherkins, sugar, paprika, Worcestershire, garlic, and mayonnaise in a bowl, and mix until well blended. Transfer the sauce to an airtight container and refrigerate until well chilled, at least 2 hours (stored in an airtight container, this sauce will keep for up to 5 days).

To cook the crabcakes, preheat the to 200 degrees F. In a non-stick (12-inch) saute pan, heat the vegetable oil over a medium high heat and saute 4 cakes at a time, browning them on each side, about 4 to 5 minutes per side. Drain the cakes on paper towels, and place them on a baking sheet in the oven to keep warm as the other crabcakes cook.

To make the fried caper flowers, heat olive oil to medium high heat in a 12-inch saute pan and fry the capers for 1 to 2 minutes, or until crisp. Drain on paper towels and use as garnish (use within 3 to 4 hours).

To serve, arrange 2 cakes on each plate and garnish with remoulade sauce, cherry tomatoes, and fried caper flowers.

JOHNNY HARRIS RESTAURANT
SHRIMP AND CRAB AU GRATIN

SERVES 6 TO 8

2 pounds small shrimp, peeled and de-veined
1 pound back-fin lump crab meat
3 cups cream sauce
2 pounds sharp cheddar cheese, shredded

CREAM SAUCE
2 pints milk
6 tablespoons butter
1 cup flour
2 teaspoons salt
2 teaspoons black pepper
1 cup cheddar cheese

To make the cream sauce, melt the butter in a heavy saucepan over medium heat. Add the flour and, using a wooden spoon, stir until all the butter is mixed into the flour. Reduce the heat and cook for 1 minute, stirring constantly. Stir in the milk all at once, and continue to stir. Cook until the sauce thickens, then add the spices and cheese. Continue to stir until the sauce is smooth and golden in color. You may add more flour to thicken, if needed.

To make the shrimp and crab au gratin, boil or steam the shrimp in a large pot of water until pink. Coat the bottom of a large casserole with cream sauce, then fold in the shrimp and crabmeat, without stirring. Add more cream sauce and put into a broiler oven at 325 degrees F until the mixture starts to bubble. Top with the cheese and return to the broiler until the cheese melts and begins to bubble. Garnish with parsley or toast points.

What started as a small barbeque shack on the corner of Bee Road and Victory Drive in 1924 has turned into a veritable Savannah icon. The business was moved to its current home in 1936 and since then has expanded to include a catering division, wine cellar, club room, private banquet rooms, and a large circular central dining room. Johnny Harris and his partner Kermit "Red" Donaldson started the business with a few Southern basics – barbeque and fried chicken. Red helped Johnny Harris to manage the business and then became a part owner in 1942 when the founder died. Later, the restaurant's famous barbeque sauce was created to accompany the popular barbecue pork, lamb, and chicken.

The large domed central dining room has a landscape mural topped by stars painted on the ceiling, and was used for decades as a ballroom for dances on special evenings. An entire hallway is covered with signed photos of celebrities that have enjoyed dining at Johnny Harris over the decades.

If you prefer to eat in a more casual atmosphere, there is an area for family-style dining that overlooks the carving area for the barbecue pork. Wherever you sit, dining at Johnny Harris is a must-see Savannah experience.

Tybee Island's Sundae Café is located on an unassuming little strip of beach businesses. Don't be fooled by the location, though. This upscale dining spot has a dynamite menu and the cozy feel of a European bistro.

Co-owners A.J. Baker and Kevin Carpenter both grew up on the island, so when they opened in 2001 they knew exactly what they wanted to create. In a few short years, their restaurant has garnered the reputation of being the best place to enjoy an upscale meal on the island. On most nights the place is so packed that it's impossible to be seated without a reservation.

The restaurant boasts some of Tybee's freshest seafood and features many local, seasonal ingredients in some new, fun dishes. Many of the entrees are sizable enough to leave you with leftovers to take home. There are a multitude of choices for dessert, many temptingly located in a cold case near the front door, so you can't possibly ignore them. If you have enough room left after your Seafood Cheesecake, try the signature dessert, a Hot Fudge Sundae!

SUNDAE CAFÉ
SEAFOOD CHEESECAKE

SERVES 6 TO 8

CRUST
6 cups Ritz Crackers, crumbled
1 cup melted butter
Pinch of salt and pepper

FILLING
1 pound grated Gouda cheese
1 cup shredded parmesan
3 pounds cream cheese (softened)
1 red onion, diced
2 green bell peppers, diced
2 roasted red peppers, diced
4 cloves garlic, diced
1 1/2 pounds shrimp, peeled and chopped
2 pounds lump crabmeat
1 tablespoon J.O. seasoning

1 tablespoon grill seasoning
1 tablespoon oregano
1 tablespoon thyme
8 eggs
1 cup heavy cream
1 cup bread crumbs

BALSAMIC SYRUP
3 cups balsamic vinegar
1/2 cup sugar

GARNISH
1 roasted red pepper, chopped
3 green onions, chopped
3 cups salad greens

To make the crust, put the Ritz Crackers in a processor to make crumbs. Mix in butter, salt, and pepper. Spray a pie pan with oil or use a pat of butter to grease the pan, and pack the crumb mixture halfway up the sides and across the bottom of the pan. Bake at 350 degrees F for 12-15 minutes.

saute onions, peppers, and garlic. Add shrimp and saute over medium heat until done. Set aside to cool. In a mixer, cream the cream cheese, eggs, and heavy cream. Add remaining ingredients, then add shrimp mixture. Finally, fold in the crabmeat. Pour into crust and bake at 325 degrees F for 45 minutes. Then cover the cheesecake with foil and bake another 45 minutes. Let cool.

To make the balsamic syrup, heat a medium saucepan over medium heat and add the vinegar and sugar. Bring to a boil and then allow to simmer for approximately 25 minutes, or until the vinegar becomes syrupy. Cool before serving.

Slice and serve on a plate garnished with the roasted red pepper and green onions, a few greens, and a drizzle of the balsamic syrup.

OLDE PINK HOUSE
SHE CRAB SOUP

SERVES 8

1/2 small onion
1 rib celery
1/4 small red pepper
8 tablespoons butter
3/4 cup all purpose flour
8 cups whole milk
1 cup Half & Half
4 ounces clam base paste (or, substitute
  1 ounce powdered fish bouillon)

1/2 ounce crab roe
1/2 teaspoon dry thyme leaves
3 dash Tabasco sauce
1/2 pound jumbo lump crab, picked of any
  shells
Kosher salt, to taste

Mince the onion, celery, and red pepper very finely. Saute the vegetables in a (4-quart) heavy saucepan on medium heat, until they are soft.

Add the flour and mix together to form a roux. Gradually add the milk, whisking continuously to avoid lumps, until all the milk is incorporated. Add the Half & Half, clam base, roe, and thyme. Continue to cook over medium-low heat, whisking often to prevent scorching, until the soup thickens and begins to gently bubble. Season with Tabasco and kosher salt to taste. Add the crab meat just before serving.

This elegant restaurant on Warren Square in downtown Savannah was once the home of James Habersham, a planter and one of the wealthiest Americans of his time. Habersham built the house in 1771, and though the exterior is now covered in pink stucco, you can still see the outline of the original brick. The story goes that for many years, each time white stucco was added to the exterior the color bled through and the stucco turned pink, so it earned the nickname "The Pink House."

The restaurant interior maintains an 18th-century feel with Venetian chandeliers, original fireplaces, and appropriate antique furniture. The tall open windows provide ample natural light during the day, and the mood is transformed during the night by the beauty of candlelight. The food matches the atmosphere, especially the traditional Low Country specialties like Shrimp with Grit Cake and the She Crab Soup.

The Planter's Tavern is the downstairs bar—complete with a cozy fireplace and the occasional jazz singer—that also serves as an alternative and more casual dining area.

FISH

Russo's Seafood has been one of the whole-sale and retail distributors of fish, shrimp, and crab to Savannah chefs and locals for more than 60 years. The owner, Charlie Russo, says that the local whiting was originally the backbone of his business, but that the restaurants in town determine which local fish is currently a popular menu item. When folks eat a great grouper dish at a local restaurant, they naturally want to create that recipe at home.

Fresh grouper, flounder, trout, shad, and red snapper have long been popular fish on local tables. Pairing the fish with local staples such as Savannah red rice, sweet potatoes, tomatoes, and crab makes for some succulent entrees, such as Sundae Café's Sweet Potato-Crusted Grouper, or Chef Joe Randall's Pan-Roasted Black Grouper with Savannah Red Rice.

It's no wonder that fishing is a major pas-time in this city, with all that you have wait-ing—just at the end of your hook.

TUBBY'S TANK HOUSE
FRIED GROUPER FINGERS

SERVES 4 TO 6

2 to 3 pounds black grouper filets
Oil for frying

BATTER
1/4 cup all-purpose flour
1 cup milk
1/2 teaspoon ground black pepper
1/2 teaspoon cayenne pepper
1/2 teaspoon salt

BREADING
2 cups all-purpose flour
1 1/2 cups cracker meal
1 tablespoon salt
1 tablespoon ground black pepper
1 teaspoon Old Bay Seafood Seasoning

To prepare the grouper fingers, cut the grouper into 1 to 2 ounce "fingers." Dredge grouper fingers in flour and shake off excess (this step helps the breading adhere to the fish).

To make the batter, mix all ingredients in a small bowl. Pour a small amount of batter into a larger bowl and coat each finger lightly with the batter mix, adding more batter to the bowl as you go.

To make the breading, combine the flour, cracker meal, salt, black pepper, and Old Bay Seafood Seasoning. Dredge the battered fingers in the breading mix and place them on wax paper until you're ready to fry.

Fry the fingers in a large skillet, with 1 inch of oil, on medium high heat until golden, about 2 minutes.

Remove from oil and drain on paper towels. Serve with lemon wedges and your choice of sauce.

Both locations of this locally owned dockhouse bar and restaurant are on the water, and both menus feature the same fried saltwater delights. The River Street Tubby's gets far more foot traffic and has a great view of the Savannah River, but the Thunderbolt location on the marshy outskirts of the city's east side is more familiar to the local population. Tubby's famous outdoor porch (complete with tree-house deck and rockers) overlooks the surrounding marshland and the Thunderbolt marina—it's a great place to kick back any day of the week.

The restaurants' owners—Ray Clark, Ansley Williams, Patrick Williams, and Sam Strickland—are committed to serving fresh seafood right off the boat. Tubby's Tankout is the most popular entree —a mixture of fried oysters, scallops, shrimp, and grouper fingers, all featuring Tubby's famous breading.

Both locations offer salads topped with seafood, chicken fingers, and a catch of the day served to your liking—grilled, blackened, or fried. Whatever location you end up visiting, you are bound to enjoy the food and fun.

"If people concentrated on the really important things in life, there'd be a shortage of fishing poles."
- Doug Larson, author

SWEET POTATO-CRUSTED GROUPER WITH PEACH CHUTNEY

SERVES 6

6 (6-8 ounce) grouper filets
1/2 cup creole mustard
1/2 cup olive oil or butter
Salt and pepper

1 pound sweet potatoes, peeled and finely grated
Oil for frying

PEACH CHUTNEY

4 ripe peaches, diced, or 1 pound. frozen peaches
1/2 yellow onion, diced
1/3 cup cran-raisins
1 green bell pepper, diced
1 teaspoon cinnamon
1/2 teaspoon cumin
1/2 teaspoon nutmeg
1/4 teaspoon ground red pepper
1/2 teaspoon ground ginger
1/4 cup apple cider vinegar
1/2 cup brown sugar

To make the chutney, saute onion and bell pepper in a saucepan over medium heat for 3 minutes. Add all remaining ingredients and simmer 10-15 minutes, stirring occasionally, until the chutney has thickened.

Grate the potatoes and set aside. Pour 2 inches of oil into a skillet, heat on high heat, and flash fry half of the grated sweet potatoes for 10 to 15 seconds. Drain on paper towels.

To prepare the grouper, heat the olive oil in a large skillet over medium heat. Salt and pepper the grouper filets and brush with creole mustard. Cover the bottom of the skillet with the other half of the grated sweet potatoes, lay the grouper filets on top, and cook until the potatoes are golden brown. Using a spatula, carefully turn the grouper and finish cooking, about 3-5 minutes.

To plate, place the grouper sweet potato-side up and top with chutney and the fried sweet potatoes. Serve with fresh sauteed spinach or a seasonal vegetable.

OLYMPIA CAFÉ
WHOLE RED SNAPPER WITH ROASTED VEGETABLES

SERVES 4

1 whole red snapper, about 4 1/2 pounds
1 cup olive oil
1/4 cup white wine
2 lemons
1 teaspoon salt
1 teaspoon pepper
1 teaspoon lemon salt
1 teaspoon paprika
1 teaspoon oregano

ROASTED VEGETABLES
1 large green pepper
1 large red pepper
2 medium zucchini
2 medium squash

2 cloves garlic, chopped
1 large onion
1/2 cup feta
1/2 cup olive oil
Salt and pepper, to taste

ROASTED POTATOES
1 dozen medium-sized red potatoes, halved
1 cup lemon juice
1 cup olive oil
2 tablespoons chicken base (powder or cubes)
1/2 tablespoon granulated garlic, optional
1 tablespoon oregano
1 tablespoon lemon pepper
Salt to taste

Blend 1/2 cup of olive oil, the juice of 2 lemons and 1/2 teaspoon salt. Reserve.

Cut 4 evenly spaced, superficial slits on the side of the snapper, making sure to cut from the head of the fish toward the tail. Repeat this process on the other side of the fish. In a deep baking pan, pour 1/2 cup olive oil over the fish, making sure that the cuts on both sides of the fish are filled with oil. Season the fish with pepper, lemon salt, paprika, oregano, and remaining salt. Pour the white wine over the fish. Pour the reserved oil mixture around the outside of the fish in the pan. Bake at 325 degrees F for 25-35 minutes, until the meat comes easily off the bone.

When the fish is done, place on a serving plate and spoon on the reserve liquid.

To bake the vegetables, slice the peppers and onion in long, thin strips. Slice zucchini and squash into rounds. Mix vegetables with the chopped garlic and place mixture in a 9x13 baking dish. Drizzle olive oil over the mixture and salt and pepper to taste. Spread the feta cheese in an even layer over the vegetables and bake at 325 degrees F for 20 minutes or until cheese starts to brown.

To roast the potatoes, wash the potatoes, halve them with peel on, and place in a shallow baking pan. Pour lemon juice and olive oil over the potatoes. In a separate pan, dissolve the chicken base in 1 1/2 cups hot water. Pour over the potatoes and sprinkle with spices and salt. Bake in a preheated oven at 350 degrees F for 30-40 minutes. If a toothpick goes easily into the potatoes, they are done.

Serve hot vegetables on a serving platter with the whole red snapper.

Year in and year out this River Street restaurant is voted the "Best Greek Food" in Savannah. Owners, Nick Pappas and Vasilis Varlagas, both natives of Greece, moved to Savannah in 1991 to pursue their dream of opening a restaurant. Olympia Café is a delight to the many guests who come to enjoy the family recipes and tasty culinary traditions of the Mediterranean. Whether it's greeting guests by name, or standing outside the front doors to offer delicious samples to passers-by, Nick and Vasilis are the consummate hosts.

Olympia Café's riverfront location is a great place to sit and watch the ferries and container ships navigate the port waters. The rustic brick floors and Greek art on the walls gives the interior the feel of a taverna on the Aegean Sea. When you visit, pay attention when a waiter shouts "OPA!" because that means that the famous flambeed cheese dish, saganaki, is being served. The café has a wide range of Greek specialties like calamari, and gyros, but don't miss the superb pizza.

PEARL'S SALTWATER GRILL
PARMESAN CRUSTED GROUPER WITH JUMBO LUMP CRABMEAT

SERVES 8

8 (6-ounce) black grouper fillets
1 pound jumbo lump crabmeat

PARMESAN CRUST
2 cups parmesan cheese, freshly grated
1 cup Panko bread crumbs
1 cup basil, roughly chopped

CITRUS BUTTER SAUCE
1/2 cup shallot, sliced
1/4 cup fresh orange juice
1/4 cup fresh lemon juice
1 cup white wine
1/2 cup heavy cream
2 sticks butter, unsalted and softened

Located on Savannah's southside near Isle of Hope, this spot is a favorite for locals who want to avoid the hustle and bustle of downtown. Many Savannahians still refer to it as just "Pearl's"—a nod to the restaurant's previous incarnation. Pearl's is a dependable spot for favorite Savannah seafood dishes, to which Chef David Weikart adds his creative touches. Plus, hush puppies come piled high in a basket before every meal. Now that's a Southern classic!

Pearl's cuisine is upscale, but the atmosphere is still casual enough to appeal to a wide range of diners. Pearl's features one of the most picturesque settings in Savannah—a panoramic view of the scenic Herb River. From their windows, you can watch marsh grass swaying, tides changing, and egrets and waterfowl in their native habitat. It's the ideal location to have a great meal and enjoy the natural beauty of the Georgia marshes.

To make the crust, combine the parmesan cheese and Panko crumbs in a food processor and pulse until well blended. Add the basil and pulse mixture until basil is finely chopped and cheese mixture has turned slightly green. Parmesan crust can be made one day ahead and refrigerated.

To make the citrus butter sauce, cook shallots, orange juice and white wine in a heavy sauce pan over medium heat until the liquid is reduced by half. Add heavy cream to the wine reduction and continue to cook until the cream thickens and small bubbles form, taking care not to brown the cream. Remove from the heat and allow the cream to cool for 2 minutes. Slowly whisk in the butter, one tablespoon at a time. Add lemon juice, salt, and white pepper to taste. Keep sauce warm until serving.

To cook the grouper, add two tablespoon of vegetable oil to a non-stick frying pan over medium heat. Put parmesan crust into a plate and press grouper fillets into the crust mixture, taking care to coat both sides. Cook both sides until golden brown, approximately 4 minutes each side. As each piece of grouper is done, place them on a sheet pan in a warm oven until you finish cooking all the grouper fillets. Quickly warm the crabmeat in frying pan—1 or 2 minutes over medium heat, at most.

Place each grouper fillet on plate and top with 2 ounces of crabmeat, then ladle the citrus butter sauce on top. Can be served with mashed potatoes or grilled asparagus.

SOHO SOUTH CAFÉ
SALMON CAKES WITH CILANTRO CREAM SAUCE

MAKES 12 CAKES

1 1/2 pounds salmon, cut into 4 or 5 pieces
1/2 cup white wine
2 teaspoons salt
3 lemon slices
Parsley

1 cup mayonnaise
1 cup fresh bread crumbs
2 eggs
2 jalapenos, finely minced
1 small yellow bell pepper, finely chopped
6 green onions, thinly sliced

1/4 cup cilantro, finely minced
2 teaspoons lemon juice
1 1/2 teaspoons salt
1/2 teaspoon cayenne pepper, or to taste
Panko, or Italian bread crumbs
Canola oil

CILANTRO CREAM SAUCE
1 cup sour cream
1/2 cup cilantro leaves
Salt and pepper to taste

To poach the salmon, create a steam bath by inserting a basket into a large pot with a tight fitting lid. Add enough water to the pot to reach the bottom of the basket, then add 1/2 cup white wine, 2 teaspoons salt, a few lemon slices and some parsley stems. Bring the water mixture to a boil and place the salmon into the basket to steam until cooked through, about 8-10 minutes, depending on the thickness of the fish. Remove the salmon, let cool, then flake the meat into 1/2-inch pieces. (If you prefer, you can season and grill the salmon, instead of poaching). Mix the remaining ingredients and fold in the flaked salmon. Shape into 12 (3-inch diameter) cakes. Dredge cakes in the Panko and saute in 1/4-inch canola oil over medium heat.

To make the Cilantro Cream, put sour cream into a processor (or use a blender, starting at slow speed and working up to "puree"). Add the cilantro leaves and mix until the cream sauce is smooth. Salt and pepper to taste.

To serve, place two crabcakes on each plate and dot the cilantro cream sauce around.

Soho South Café has all the eclecticism and fun, funky style of its famous namesake Manhattan art district. The open dining area was formerly an old auto repair shop and has been converted to suggest the feel of a large artist's loft. Owner Bonnie Retsas opened the restaurant in 1997 after moving from New York to Savannah, and Soho South attracts as many art lovers as food lovers.

Soho South's motto, "Where Food is an Art," is clearly reflected in their creative menu. The light lunch items – panini, soups, salads, and entrees – incorporate flavors that range from Middle Eastern to European, to good ole' fashioned country cooking. Everything is prepared with fresh and healthy ingredients. Be prepared to come early to get a table, because this historic district eatery is always buzzing with hungry tourists and locals.

UNCLE BUBBA'S OYSTER HOUSE
CRAB STUFFED FLOUNDER

SERVES 6

6 (10-ounce) flounder fillets
1 1/2 teaspoon salt
1 1/2 teaspoons freshly ground black pepper
Uncle Bubba's Crab Cake Mix, recipe follows
1 1/2 teaspoons paprika
Cooking spray
6 (1-inch) slices Crab Butter, recipe follows
Fresh parsley, for garnish

CRAB CAKE MIX
1 1/2 tablespoons butter
3 green onions, green tops, thinly sliced
1 clove garlic, minced
1 teaspoon fresh parsley leaves, chopped
1 small green pepper, finely chopped
1 egg
1/8 teaspoon cayenne pepper

1/8 teaspoon garlic powder
3 tablespoons heavy cream
1 1/2 tablespoons spicy mustard
1/2 lemon, juiced
2 tablespoons mayonnaise
10 saltine crackers, crumbled medium to fine
1/2 pound lump crabmeat, picked clean of
  shells
1/2 pound claw crabmeat, picked clean of
  shells
Salt and freshly ground black pepper

CRAB BUTTER
1 ounce claw crabmeat, picked clean of shells
1 stick unsalted butter, softened
1/2 tablespoon seafood base
1/2 green onion, thinly sliced

To make the crab cake mix, melt the butter in a medium skillet and saute the onions, garlic, parsley, and peppers until soft. Let cool to room temperature.

In a mixing bowl, combine the sauteed vegetable mixture, egg, cayenne pepper, garlic powder, heavy cream, mustard, lemon juice, and mayonnaise together. Gently mix in the saltine crackers and crabmeat. Add salt and pepper, if needed. Set aside to stuff in flounder.

To make the crab butter, fold the crab, butter, seafood base, and onions together in a medium bowl and mix until smooth. Remove from the bowl and shape into a log on a piece of parchment paper. Roll up and place in the freezer. Reserve for flounder.

Preheat the oven to 350 degrees F.

Sprinkle flounder with salt and pepper. Using a fillet knife, carefully open the flounder by cutting along the left and right sides of the seam down the middle of the fish to make pockets. Lay the cut sides back. Stuff each flounder with 4 ounces of the Crab Cake Mix, and press the sides down to cover the filling. Sprinkle with paprika.

Coat a glass baking dish with cooking spray. Place the fish in the dish and bake for 20 minutes. Without removing the dish from the oven, turn the oven to broil and broil for 5 additional minutes.

To serve, put a hot fillet on each plate, place a medallion of crab butter on top of the grilled fish, and sprinkle with fresh parsley for added color.

Uncle Bubba's Oyster House belongs to the brother of Savannah celebrity chef, Paula Deen, and you can expect the same great home cooking and enthusiastic crowds at this Whitemarsh Island restaurant as those at Paula's Lady & Sons restaurant downtown.

Originally, Paula and Bubba Deen wanted to open a restaurant near Savannah. After plans to open the restaurant in a Charleston location didn't pan out, Deen got a call from a close friend about a spot on Turner's Creek that was going out of business. The opportunity was just what the sister-brother duo was looking for, and they quickly went to work building Uncle Bubba's Oyster House.

In a few short years the restaurant gained a loyal following, and in 2008 was named "Best Seafood Restaurant" by Savannah Magazine. The restaurant is designed to look, smell, and taste like a good old-fashioned oyster roast right on the water. The space even features an oyster pit in the middle—all part of Bubba's plan to feed friends and family great food in a comfortable family atmosphere.

CHEF JOE RANDALL'S
PAN-ROASTED BLACK GROUPER

SERVES 8

1/2 teaspoon salt
1/2 teaspoon freshly ground black pepper
8 (4-ounce) black grouper fillets
2 tablespoons olive oil
6 tablespoons melted butter
2 tablespoons fresh lemon juice
1/4 cup fresh chives, chopped

SAVANNAH RED RICE
1/8 pound salt pork, finely diced
1/2 cup red bell pepper, diced
1/2 cup green bell pepper, diced
1/4 cup celery, diced

1 cup onions, diced
2 teaspoons garlic, minced
1/4 pound smoked sausage, diced
2 cups long-grain white rice
2 cups crushed canned whole tomatoes,
    drained
2 tablespoons tomato paste
3 1/2 cups water
1/2 teaspoon salt
1/4 teaspoon freshly ground black pepper
1/2 teaspoon cayenne pepper

Season the grouper with salt and black pepper. Heat 2 tablespoons melted butter in a large skillet. Cook in three batches to avoid overcrowding in the pan. Adding olive oil as needed, sear and turn the grouper, cooking about 3 minutes. Place a pan with all the fillets in a 400 degree F oven for 3 to 5 minutes.

To make the red rice, heat a large heavy-bottomed saucepan and cook the salt pork until crisp. Add the red and green peppers, celery, onions, garlic, and sausage and continue to cook for 3 to 4 minutes. Add the rice and stir, coating the rice with the drippings. Stir in the tomatoes, tomato paste, water, salt, black and cayenne peppers. Cover and simmer for 25-30 minutes, or until rice is tender and liquid is absorbed.

To plate, place the grouper over a round of rice, garnish with fresh chopped chives, and serve immediately.

Widely known as both a caterer and teacher, Chef Joe Randall won't ever hesitate to offer some wisdom about the rich culinary traditions of the South. Although Randall grew up in the North, he moved to Georgia to master the techniques and styles of African-American cuisine in the South. Randall is now one of the foremost proponents of maintaining the culinary heritage handed down by other well-known African-American chefs. His book, A Taste of Heritage, *is filled with many of the idioms and recipes that have made Southern cooking so enduring. Randall offers training in this culinary heritage at his cooking school, which opened its doors in 2000.*

In the comfort of his kitchen, the award-winning chef creates an atmosphere where it is easy to learn the arts of Southern cooking. Chef Randall says his mission is to "put a little South in your mouth and joy back into your kitchen."

DRIFTAWAY CAFE
PAN-SEARED RED SNAPPER

Southside Savannah residents have really taken a shine to this café in the Sandfly community. Chef Kirk Blaine is Savannah born and raised, but he trained at New York's prestigious Culinary Institute of America, so he brings the best of both culinary worlds to his table. Under the direction of owners Robyn and Michelle Quattlebaum, Driftaway Cafe is turning heads with its inventive twists on Savannah's local seafood.

The restaurant provides casual coastal cuisine that appeals to a wide range of people, but it's always a first-class dining experience. The large front porch is popular for the lunch and brunch crowd, and the decor is decidedly maritime.

If you are a meat-lover, there are plenty of options, including the hand cut steaks and prime rib; however, the restaurant shines with its saltwater specials, inventively mixed with Asian, Latin, and continental flavors.

SERVES 4

4 (6-8 ounce) snapper filets, scales removed, skin on
4 tablespoons olive oil
Salt and pepper

PESTO
1/2 cup of toasted Valdosta pecans
1/2 cup sweet basil, preferably locally grown
1/2 cup fresh grated Parmesan cheese
4 cloves garlic
3 tablespoons extra virgin olive oil
1 teaspoon kosher salt
1 teaspoon ground black pepper

1 teaspoon granulated sugar
1 teaspoon cayenne pepper
1 teaspoon cumin powder

PROVENCAL TOMATOES
1 pint cherry tomatoes, halved
2 teaspoons fresh chopped garlic
2 teaspoons olive oil
1 cup of dry white wine
2 tablespoons butter
2 teaspoons chopped parsley
Pinch of salt and pepper

To make the pesto, mix all ingredients into a food processor and blend until smooth. This step can be done a day ahead to allow the garlic flavor to mellow. Leftover pesto can be refrigerated and used for a month.

To make the Provencal tomatoes, heat the olive oil in a saute pan and add the tomatoes. Salt and pepper them, and cook for 1-2 minutes over medium-high heat, or until the edges have a little color. Add the garlic to the saute pan, then immediately add the wine so that the garlic doesn't burn. Bring the mixture to a full boil for about 4 minutes, or until all of the extra water has evaporated from the wine. Remove from the heat and add the whole butter and parsley, stirring until the sauce thickens.

To prepare the snapper, score the skin, taking care not to cut deeply into the meat. Season the fish on both sides with salt and pepper. Heat a pan over high heat, and place the snapper skin side down in the pan, pressing the fish flat to prevent the skin from curling up. You may also place a small plate on the top of the fish to flatten it. This process ensures that the fish has crispy skin, and cooks evenly and quickly. Cook the skin side of the snapper for about 5 minutes, then flip the filet, and finish cooking on the other side for about one minute.

To plate the fish, add a dab of the pesto, the Provencal tomatoes, and a seasonal vegetable, such as asparagus.

Savannah's marshes and creeks are not only inland waterways, but home to many fish and fowl.

OYSTERS

The 18th-century satirist Jonathan Swift wrote, "He was a bold man that first ate an oyster." And, I would add, he must inevitably have been a happy one!

As their beds are revealed at low tide, it becomes evident that oysters are abundant throughout Savannah and the Low Country. Savannahians have long enjoyed a surfeit of recipes featuring the distinctive texture and sweetness of this native mullosk. Bluffton oysters are the prized choice of local cooks.

The winter oyster roast is a time-honored celebration for locals, and the best time to harvest them. In a custom that hasn't changed in centuries, great quantities of oysters are roasted in water-soaked burlap bags over an open fire until the shells pop open. Steaming oysters are thrown onto rough-hewn tables and guests are supplied with gloves and oyster knives to extract the little beauties.

Savannahians know how to enjoy both seafood and the outdoors, even in winter!

Mrs. Wilkes' Boardinghouse Restaurant
Confederates on Horseback

SERVES 6, AS AN APPETIZER

2 pints select oysters
12 slices of bacon, halved
1/2 teaspoon salt
1/8 teaspoon pepper
1/8 teaspoon paprika
2 tablespoons parsley, finely chopped
Lemon wedges

Wash and drain the oysters and lay each oyster across half a slice of bacon. Mix the salt, pepper, paprika, and parsley and sprinkle onto the oysters. Roll bacon around each oyster and spear with a toothpick to hold in place during baking. Place in a shallow baking pan on the lower rack of the oven and bake at 450 degrees F for about 10 minutes, or until bacon is crisp.

Remove picks and serve hot with lemon wedges.

Named after its founder, Mrs. Wilkes' Boardinghouse Restaurant has been a Savannah destination for more than 65 years. Though Wilkes passed away in 2003, her family continues serving her tried-and-true recipes to scores of daily diners in the boardinghouse-style. The restaurant was named one of the "50 Most Distinguished Restaurants in the United States" by Condé Nast Traveler, *as well as receiving a James Beard medal in 2000, and many other awards and accolades.*

Offering some of the city's best Southern food, including fried chicken and biscuits, the restaurant serves lunch on weekdays and is available for private functions at other times. After patiently waiting in the line that forms early mornings along Jones Street, visitors are directed inside to large communal tables, where it is common to meet visitors from around the world who've all come to experience Mrs. Wilkes' food. Once seated, patrons don't have to worry about ordering from a menu, because whatever is cooking that day will be passed around the table in generous portions.

Though most guests are full at the end of the hearty meal, no one can seem to resist the delicious desert offerings, especially the enduring favorite—Southern banana pudding.

Martha Giddens Nesbit's
Oyster Dressing

SERVES 12

3/4 cup butter
1 cup chopped celery
1/4 cup finely chopped onion
4 pieces of toast, made into crumbs in food processor
5 cups crumbled corn bread (use a mix, such as buttermilk mix)
1 teaspoon salt
1 1/2 teaspoons pepper
1 1/2 teaspoons poultry seasoning

3 cups chicken or turkey broth
4 eggs, beaten
1 pint oysters, drained and picked through for shells

It would be hard to find anyone who knows as much about Savannah's food scene and culinary history as Martha Giddens Nesbit. Martha has written books on entertaining in Savannah, food columns for the city's newspaper and Savannah magazine, and has co-authored several books with Paula Deen. She has also appeared on a Food Network special with Bobby Flay featuring some of Savannah's most famous food personalities.

As a caterer, Martha really knows how to use the best of what is in season in Savannah, and she is a virtual encyclopedia of knowledge on Low Country recipes and techniques. Having been a food writer for over 30 years, she also knows all of the city's best dishes and the restaurants where you can enjoy them. With all of this knowledge and experience under her belt, it's no surprise that she throws legendary dinner parties with classic dishes and mouth-watering desserts.

Melt butter in a heavy skillet. saute the celery and onion until soft over low heat, about 5-7 minutes. In a large mixing bowl, combine the sauteed vegetables, toast crumbs, crumbled corn bread and seasonings. Stir in about 2 cups of broth and the eggs. The mixture should be very loose, but not soupy. Add more broth if necessary. Gently stir in the oysters.

Place the dressing in a 9-by-13-inch casserole dish sprayed with vegetable cooking spray. Make sure no oysters are exposed. Bake uncovered at 350 degrees F for 40 to 45 minutes, until casserole is "set" and puffed.

Serve with a holiday turkey and all the trimmings.

CAFE 37
OYSTER STEW

SERVES 6

12 large carrots
14 stalks celery
6 large onions
2 tablespoons chopped garlic
4 tablespoons fresh thyme
1 bunch parsley, chopped and stems reserved
2 tablespoons canola oil
4 cups heavy cream
1 quart large oysters, rinsed
1 cup diced tasso ham
2 cups unoaked white wine
sourdough bread, sliced and toasted

Roughly chop half the carrots, onion, and celery and put into a 4 quart stock pot with 2 quarts of water, and the thyme and parsley stems. Simmer for 45 minutes to reduce the liquid by half. Strain and reserve the remaining 1 quart liquid, and reserve.

Chop the remaining carrots, onion, and celery into 1/4-inch dice, and put into a 4-quart pot over low heat and add the canola oil. Cook for 15 minutes, until the vegetables are softened.

Stir in the chopped garlic, add the wine, and cook until almost all the liquid is evaporated. Add the reserved vegetable stock and simmer for 15 minutes, then add heavy cream and simmer another 5 minutes. This stock can be refrigerated until you are ready to serve the stew.

When you are ready to serve the stew, bring the stock to barely simmering (if it's been refrigerated and needs warming), then salt and pepper to taste. Add the oysters, tasso ham, and chopped parsley to the stew and cook over low heat for 2-3 minutes, or until oysters are just cooked. Adjust the salt and pepper if needed, and serve with toasted sourdough bread.

"Oysters are the most tender and delicate of all seafoods. They stay in bed all day and night. They never work or take exercise, are stupendous drinkers, and wait for their meals to come to them."
- Hector Bolitho,
The Glorious Oyster

CAFE 37
OYSTER PO' BOY

SERVES 6

1 quart large shucked oysters
2 cups buttermilk
2 eggs
2 cups yellow cornmeal
2 cups all purpose flour
1 tablespoon kosher salt

REMOULADE
1 cup mayonnaise
1/4 cup capers
1 bunch flat leaf parsley, chopped
1 tablespoon Worcestershire sauce
1 tablespoon lemon juice
1 head iceberg lettuce, thinly shredded

12 slices sourdough bread, toasted
Peanut oil for frying

Combine all remoulade ingredients together in a bowl, whisk until well mixed, and set aside.

Heat oil in a deep, cast iron pan with a wire strainer basket to 375 degrees F. (It's useful to have a thermometer for frying to make sure the oil stays hot enough.)

To make the oyster batter, whisk together the eggs and buttermilk. In another bowl, mix the cornmeal, flour, and salt. Drain the oysters, coat with the buttermilk mixture, then coat well with the flour mixture. Place the battered oysters in the strainer basket and shake off the excess flour. Cook oysters in the hot oil for 3 to 4 minutes. Remove and drain oysters on paper towels.

Dress each piece of bread with the remoulade sauce, and top one side with lettuce and one with oysters and serve.

Tucked behind an antique store on 37th Street is one of Savannah's hottest new restaurants. Cafe 37 isn't large (only eight tables), but the dining area is filled with natural light and a comfortable coziness. The restaurant opened in 2008 and has created quite a buzz since then. In the beginning, the restaurant served a limited menu for lunch, but now that their reputation has grown, they serve dinner three nights a week. Thursday is my personal favorite for dinner, as the menu offers a choice of small plates, which change weekly. On Fridays and Saturdays there are daily specials—including a fresh catch and homemade pastas.

The Chef and Owner, Blake Elsinghorst, is familiar with Savannah as a graduate of the Savannah College of Art and Design. His cooking has a strong French influence, which he acquired when he attended culinary school in France. Although Elsinghorst doesn't do many Southern dishes, his delicious version of Savannah's most famous seafood sandwich, the Oyster Po' Boy, earns high marks among Savannahians.

"I prefer my oysters fried.
That way I know my
oysters died."

- Roy Blount, Jr., author

Pearl's Saltwater Grill
Cornmeal Fried Oysters

SERVES 6

2 cups yellow cornmeal
1 tablespoon Cajun Seasoning
1 cup buttermilk
1 quart select oysters, drained
1 lemon
Vegetable oil

HORSERADISH SOUR CREAM SAUCE
1/2 cup prepared horseradish
1/2 cup sour cream
1/2 cup mayonnaise
1 tablespoon Worcestershire sauce
1 teaspoon Tabasco sauce
1 teaspoon salt
1 teaspoon black pepper

Parsley, for garnish

To make the horseradish sour cream sauce, combine all ingredients in a mixing bowl and chill. This sauce also goes well with steaks, potatoes, and blackened fish.

To fry the oysters, first combine the cornmeal and Cajun spice in a big bowl. Soak the oysters in buttermilk for one minute. Drain the oysters and completely coat them in the cornmeal mixture, leaving them in the cornmeal for one minute. Heat 2 inches of oil to 350 degrees F in a large skillet. Shake off excess cornmeal and fry oysters until golden brown, for 2 minutes. Drain oysters on a plate with a dish towel or paper towels.

To serve, spoon horseradish sauce onto plate and top with fried oysters. Garnish with lemon wedges and parsley.

BLOODY MARY OYSTER SHOOTERS

SERVES 6

"*Good food is a showcase of talent. Great food is a showcase of passion.*"
- Michael Kenny,
Savor... Savannah Catering

6 large freshly shucked Bluffton oysters, rinsed

BLOODY MARY MIX
9 ounces V-8 Juice
1 teaspoon prepared horseradish
2 teaspoons Tabasco
1 1/2 ounces vodka
1 lemon (cut into small slices)
3 tablespoons Old Bay Seasoning

Use 6 (3-ounce) cordial glasses, each rimmed with Old Bay Seasoning.

In a mixing bowl, combine tomato juice, horseradish, and Tabasco. Mix thoroughly and set aside.

Place one oyster in each shot glass and add Bloody Mary mixture until glass is 3/4 full. Add 1/4 ounce of vodka to each glass and garnish with a lemon slice.

The shooters can be prepared ahead and refrigerated for up to two hours.

I do not weep at the world—I am too busy sharpening my oyster knife.

- Zora Neale Hurston

OLDE PINK HOUSE
FRIED OYSTER CAESAR SALAD

SERVES 8

DRESSING
1/4 cup red wine vinegar
1/3 cup grated Parmegianno Reggiano cheese
1 teaspoon Dijon mustard
2 anchovy fillets
1 clove garlic
1 egg yolk
1/2 teaspoon Tabasco sauce
4 teaspoons Worcestershire sauce
1 teaspoon ground black pepper
1 cup olive oil (not Extra Virgin, Pomace is best)

CROUTONS
1 small baguette
1/4 cup olive oil
1 teaspoon garlic powder
1 teaspoon dry thyme
1 teaspoon dry basil

CHEESE CRISPS
1/2 cup grated Parmeggiano Reggiano cheese

SALAD
3 whole Romaine hearts
1 cup croutons
8 cheese crisps

FRIED OYSTERS
40 shucked oysters
2 cups all-purpose flour, seasoned well with salt and pepper
1 cup Caesar dressing

To make the dressing, blend all ingredients except for the oil in a food processor. Slowly drizzle in olive oil until fully incorporated. If you do not have a food processor, finely mince the garlic and anchovies and put in a large bowl with all other ingredients except the oil. Briskly whisk everything together, and while whisking, slowly drizzle in the oil until fully incorporated.

To make the croutons, cut the baguette into 1/2-inch squares, mix with rest of ingredients, and bake on a sheet pan at 350 degrees F until crisp.

To make the cheese crisps, line a large sheet pan with parchment paper, and place 8 heaping tablespoons of the cheese, leaving as much space as possible in between. Flatten the cheese into 3" diameter circles and bake in a 325 degree F oven until the cheese is melted and bubbly. Remove from oven and cool completely before removing the crisps from the pan with a spatula.

Cut the Romaine into bite size pieces and chill.

In a deep casserole or cast iron pan, heat 2 inches of cooking oil to 350 degrees F (or use a deep fryer if you have one). Dust the oysters in the seasoned flour and cook in the hot oil approximately 3 minutes, or until oyster are crispy. Keep the oysters warm while you make the salad.

In a large bowl, mix the lettuce with the Caesar dressing.

To plate, place a small amount of lettuce in the center of the plate. Arrange 5 oysters around the lettuce on each plate. Place a cheese crisp on top and top that with additional lettuce. Garnish with a few croutons and serve.

MARTHA GIDDENS NESBIT
SCALLOPED OYSTERS

SERVES 6 TO 8

1 pint shucked oysters, drained and picked
  through for shells
2 cups oyster crackers, crumbled
1/4 cup melted butter
1/2 teaspoon salt
1/2 teaspoon pepper
1 cup Half & Half
1 tablespoon sherry
Dash hot sauce
1 teaspoon Worcestershire sauce

"Savannah tastes like tiny, salty oysters, roasted over an open fire with water-soaked burlap bags. The leftovers become stew or scalloped oysters, a simple dish of oysters, butter and crushed saltine crackers."
- Martha Giddens
Nesbit

Spray a 9-inch round casserole dish with vegetable cooking spray. In a medium-sized mixing bowl, combine the cracker crumbs and butter. Stir to combine. Use your fingers if necessary to make sure all the crumbs are coated.

Using half the buttered crumbs, arrange a layer of crumbs to cover the bottom of the dish.

Layer the oysters on top of the crumb mixture. Season with salt and pepper, and top with the remaining crumbs, making sure to cover all of the oysters.

Combine the Half & Half, sherry, hot sauce, and Worcestershire. Pour evenly over crumbs.

Bake in a 400 degree F oven for 20 minutes, until liquid is absorbed, and serve hot as a side dish.

SHRIMP

If you want to enjoy panoramic views of the Atlantic, within sight of shrimp boats netting their daily haul, the pier at Tybee beach is a good spot to be. Decoratively painted with an underwater mural, the pier and pavilion is the favorite spot for picnics and parties. Tybrisa (the original Indian name for the island) Pier is a favorite spot for fishermen and "beach bums"—a term that Tybee-ites fondly use to refer to themselves. If you're lucky enough to be on Tybee for the Beach Bums parade at the end of May, you'll be witness to and participant in the most fun anyone—child or adult—can have with a watergun.

A visitor crossing the bridge over Lazaretto Creek to Tybee Island will often see a fleet of local shrimpboats docked at the Lazaretto Creek marina. If you're lucky enough to catch the shrimpboats returning in the afternoon with their haul, it's great fun to watch the shrimpers emptying their nets—it's a surefire way to work up an appetite.

Kayak Kafé
Watermelon and Wild Georgia Shrimp Salad

SERVES 4 TO 6

16-20 cups loosely packed organic mixed
  greens
2 pounds medium wild Georgia shrimp
  (or fresh local substitute), shells on
1/4 cup Old Bay Seasoning
2 cups seedless watermelon, cut into
  1 1/2-inch cubes
1/2 red onion, julienned
1 1/2 cups crumbled feta cheese
1/2 cup fresh lime juice

1/4 cup champagne vinegar
1/2 cup extra virgin olive oil
1/4 cup chopped cilantro
1 garlic clove, minced
Salt and pepper to taste
Cayenne pepper, for garnish
Lime wedges, for garnish

Bring 6 quarts of water to a rolling boil and add Old Bay Seasoning. Add raw shrimp to the water and cook until firm, about 4 minutes.

Strain and cool shrimp in an ice water bath. Peel and clean shrimp and put into a large mixing bowl. Add mixed greens, cubed watermelon, julienned red onion, cilantro, and garlic to bowl. Drizzle with lime juice, vinegar, and olive oil and toss. Salt and pepper to taste.

To plate, distribute salad evenly on cold plates. Sprinkle crumbled feta on each salad, garnish with a lime wedge, and lightly dust with cayenne pepper. Serve cold.

Located on the main street of Savannah's downtown historic district, this trendy café on Broughton Street is buzzing every weekday around lunchtime. Kayak Kafé offers healthy fare to business people and tourists who want to enjoy quick eats in a casual environment. The Kafé is fittingly located in the same building as the Downtown Athletic Club, so club members can get a workout and a light meal afterward. The outdoor tables are a great spot for people-watching on this busy street.

Kayak Kafé consistently wins Connect Savannah's *reader award for "Best Salad," and it's no surprise considering they use fresh organic greens and vine-ripe tomatoes from Polk's Fresh Market. They also serve daily specials, soups, and sandwiches on a variety of multi-grain breads. If it's seafood you crave, try one of their items that feature Wild Georgia Shrimp. One of my favorites is this cool seasonal treat—Shrimp and Watermelon Salad!*

THE CRAB SHACK
CAPT'N CRAB'S LOW COUNTRY BOIL

SERVES 8

1/2 cup Capt'n Crab's Secret Spice
  (or any seafood seasoning)
1/4 cup salt
4 tablespoons black pepper
1/4 cup white vinegar
2 pounds new potatoes, quartered
2 pounds smoked sausage links, cut into
  1-inch pieces
8 ears corn, cut into 2-inch pieces
1/2 onion (optional), cut in thick slices
3 pounds fresh shrimp, tails on

Fill a 16-quart pot with 8 quarts water. Bring water to a rolling boil and add the Secret Spice, salt, pepper and vinegar. Add new potatoes and cook for 5 minutes. Add the sausage and corn (and onion), and continue cooking for 10 minutes or until the potatoes are tender. Turn the burner off and add the shrimp, letting them cook for 2 minutes (they will float and shell on the tail will separate from the meat).

Drain the water, sprinkle with Capt'n Crab's Secret Spice to taste, and serve with lemon wedges, cocktail sauce, and plenty of paper towels.

The Crab Shack's original tag line, "Where the Elite Eat in Their Bare Feet," says it all about this Tybee Island dockside restaurant and bar—it has rightfully gained a reputation for its laid-back approach to dining and seafood "so fresh you want to slap it." It's the perfect spot to kick off your shoes and unwind with a cold drink after a long day on the water, or bring the kids for lunch or dinner to enjoy the playground atmosphere.

The spot along Chimney Creek where the restaurant lies actually used to be an old fishing camp. In 1983, owners Jack and Belinda Flanagan were living in Atlanta and saw an ad for the property in the paper. They decided to trade in their hectic lives in the city for a peaceful adventure on the coast, and the rest is history.

What started as a few tables on the marsh serviced by a small kitchen is now a sprawling complex of decks, screened-in dining areas, a marina, an aviary, a gift shop, a bar, and a gator pit where guests can check out hundreds of live alligators. Consistently voted the "Best Seafood" and "Best Outdoor Dining in Savannah," the Crab Shack is easily the most fun you can have dining out on the island.

SUSAN MASON CATERING
PICKLED SHRIMP

SERVES 8 TO 10

1/2 cup celery tops
1/4 cup pickling spice
4 pounds jumbo shrimp, peeled, deveined,
    and tails removed
3 1/2 teaspoons salt

PICKLING MIXTURE
3 stalks celery, chopped
2 large white onions, thinly sliced
1 1/4 cups vegetable oil
3/4 cup apple cider vinegar
2 1/2 teaspoons salt
8 bay leaves
2 1/2 tablespoons capers, packed in vinegar
6 drops Tabasco sauce
1/2 green bell pepper, seeded, de-ribbed,
    and diced

To cook the shrimp, tie the celery tops and pickling spice in a cheesecloth bag. Bring a large pot of water to a boil over high heat. Place the cheesecloth bag in the water, decrease the heat to medium-low, and simmer for 10 minutes. Add the shrimp and salt and simmer for 5 minutes, or until the shrimp are pink all over. Drain.

To pickle the shrimp, combine all the pickling ingredients and the shrimp in a large, non-reactive bowl. Cover and refrigerate for 12 hours. Drain, discard the pickling mixture, and serve the shrimp cold on a silver platter or in a decorative ceramic bowl.

It is hard to think of any other Savannah personality who embodies fine Southern hospitality as much as Susan Mason. Although she was born in Alabama, Susan epitomizes the grace and elegance that Savannah parties are so well known for, and we have long claimed her as our own.

The catering business, which she runs from her exquisitely decorated Victorian home and a kitchen storefront in nearby Ardsley Park, has been voted the best in Savannah for many years running. Her trademark silver platters, strawberry trees, and elegant, upscale dinners set the standard for parties in Savannah and around the Low Country.

Susan got her sense of hospitality from her upbringing in the South, but her cooking style was greatly complemented by European culinary and cultural influences that she acquired on yearly visits to Provence, France. The combination of elegant cuisine and a warm personality has served Susan well over the years. In fact, her parties are so memorable that she has built her business completely on word-of-mouth advertising. Her cookbook, Susan Mason's Silver Service, *is a scrumptious testament to her style and her fabulous food.*

North Beach Grill
Caribbean-Spiced Boiled Shrimp

SERVES 4

1 pound medium shrimp (shell on)
2 tablespoons fresh garlic, chopped
2 tablespoons fresh ginger, chopped
1 large jalapeno, seeded and julienned
1 tablespoon peppercorns
1 teaspoon salt
3 tablespoons olive oil
2 tablespoons butter

2 tablespoons orange juice (with pulp)
Juice of 1 lemon
4 tablespoons concentrated grape juice
2 tablespoons grapefruit juice
2 tablespoons pineapple juice

1 mango, sliced
1/2 pineapple, sliced

Visit the historic lighthouse on the North side of Tybee Island, and you might be surprised to find this hip hangout just a few hundred yards away. The North Beach Grill started out as a tiny watering hole in 1993, and is now one of the highlights of the island—voted "Best Tybee Restaurant" by Connect Savannah *readers in 2008, and the recipient of reviews in newspapers and magazines all along the east coast. The indoor dining area features the bar and a large dining room, or you can sit on the outdoor patio if you want to drink and dine in bathing suits and flip flops.*

Chef and owner George Spriggs infuses his seafood dishes with a Caribbean flair, which is mirrored by the mellow reggae tunes frequently played on the grill's sound system, or by the occasional patio band during the summer. In fact, after enjoying some of George's famous plantains with a cold daiquiri, you might just think that you are in Key West or the Caymans instead of the Georgia coast.

Blend orange, lemon, grape, grapefruit, and pineapple juices together and set aside.

In a large saute pan combine the garlic, ginger, peppercorns, jalapeno, and olive oil and heat over medium heat. saute until the garlic begins to toast, then stir in the shrimp. Add salt and butter. As the shrimp begin to turn pink, add the juice mixture. Continue to cook over a medium heat to reduce the liquid by half and fully cook the shrimp, about 12 minutes.

Serve hot and garnish with slices of mango and pineapple.

MRS. WILKES' BOARDINGHOUSE RESTAURANT
SEAFOOD CASSEROLE

SERVES 6

1/2 cup green pepper, chopped
1/2 cup onion, finely chopped
1 cup celery, chopped
1/2 cup pimento, chopped
1 (10-ounce) can mushroom soup
1 (4-ounce) can mushrooms
1 cup mayonnaise
8 tablespoons butter
1/2 teaspoon salt
1/2 teaspoon pepper
1 tablespoon lemon juice
1 tablespoon Worcestershire sauce
1 cup milk

3 cups cooked rice
1 cup mild cheddar cheese, grated
1 pound crab meat, claw
1 pound shrimp, cooked

Lemon wedges

Saute the green pepper, onion, and celery in butter. Combine the rest of the ingredients, except for the cheese, add the sauteed vegetables and mix well. Pour into a 3-quart casserole dish and top with the grated cheese. Bake in a 350 degrees F oven for 45 minutes.

Serve the casserole in your best serving dish and offer lemon wedges on the side.

May the holes in your net be no larger than the fish in it.

\- Irish Blessing

17Hundred90
Shrimp and Onion Quiche

SERVES 6

1 medium yellow onion, julienned
3/4 teaspoon kosher salt
1/2 teaspoon black pepper
4 eggs
1/4 cup olive oil
3/4 cup Half & Half
1 1/2 cups shredded cheddar cheese
1/2 pound shrimp (extra small), shell off
1 (9-inch) piecrust, in tin

Named for the year in which it was built, this historic inn is the oldest in the city. Just off Columbia Square, 17Hundred90 maintains the historic atmosphere of an 18th century inn by preserving its old brick floors, antique fireplaces, and period decor. In addition to the authentic historic atmosphere, it is also reported to be the home of one of the city's many ghosts: a seaman's mistress, Anna Powers, who is said to reside in room 204.

The restaurant has stood the test of time, and has been serving some of the finest food Savannah has to offer for more than a century. Their menu is a gourmet interpretation of authentic Savannah cuisine, and the dining area is the perfect place to enjoy fine dining in a traditional setting. With all of its history and charm, it's no surprise that Gourmet Magazine *celebrated it as "the most elegant restaurant in Savannah."*

Preheat the oven to 350 degrees F.

In a large bowl, beat the eggs and add the salt, pepper, and Half & Half.

saute the shrimp in olive oil for 1- 2 minutes on both sides over medium heat. Set aside. saute onions for 1 minute over medium heat until onions start to glisten. Add the shrimp and onions to the egg mixture and stir. Pour into the unbaked pie shell, sprinkle cheese on top, and bake for 25 minutes. Let stand for 10 minutes before slicing.

Serve with a side salad for a great lunch or brunch.

THE LADY & SONS
CRAB-STUFFED SHRIMP

SERVES 4

1 tablespoon butter
3 green onions, finely chopped
1/2 cup green bell pepper, finely chopped
1/4 teaspoon garlic powder
4 1/2 teaspoons heavy cream
1 tablespoon Dijon mustard
Dash cayenne pepper
1/2 cup saltine cracker crumbs
1/4 cup mayonnaise
1 egg
2 tablespoons fresh parsley leaves
1/2 lemon, juiced
1 pound crabmeat, picked over
1 pound extra-large or jumbo shrimp, peeled,
    deveined, tails on
12 slices bacon, halved crosswise
2 cups steamed white rice, optional

ROUX
1 stick butter
1 cup all-purpose flour

BASIL CREAM SAUCE
2 tablespoons butter
1 tablespoon olive oil
1 teaspoon minced garlic
1/2 cup diced onions
1/4 cup white wine
1/2 quart heavy cream
1 teaspoon chicken base
2 tablespoons pesto (recipe follows)
1 teaspoon Roux (recipe follows)

PESTO
2 cups fresh basil leaves
1 cup walnut pieces
1 cup grated Parmesan cheese
1 teaspoon minced garlic
1 cup olive oil

To make the pesto, blend all ingredients in a food processor until a coarse paste is formed. Place in an airtight container and refrigerate until ready to use. Yields about 1 1/2 cups

To make the Roux, melt the butter in a large skillet over medium-low heat. Slowly add the flour and stir until lightly browned. Leftover roux can be stored, refrigerated and tightly covered, for several weeks.

Melt butter in a skillet over medium heat and cook the green onions, green pepper, and garlic powder until peppers are limp. Place the mixture in a large bowl and add the cream, mustard, and cayenne pepper and mix well. Add cracker crumbs, mayonnaise, egg, parsley, and lemon juice and mix. Gently fold in the crabmeat. Form the mixture into small patties to stuff into the shrimp. Set aside.

To prepare the shrimp, split the shrimp down the bottom center to the tail, being careful not to cut through. Stuff each shrimp with the crabmeat mixture. Wrap shrimp in bacon and secure with a toothpick. Place on a baking pan and cook at 350 degrees F until the bacon is crisp and the shrimp are pink, about 15-20 minutes.

To make the basil cream sauce, heat the butter and olive oil in a skillet over medium heat. Add garlic and onion and cook until lightly browned, about 5 minutes. Add white wine and reduce by half. Add heavy cream and chicken stock and reduce by half again. Add pesto and roux, bring to a simmer and heat until slightly thickened, about 2 to 3 minutes.

To serve, arrange 6 shrimp on a bed of rice, drizzle with the basil cream sauce, and serve.

If you ask people outside the South what makes Paula Deen famous, they might cite her Food Network shows, her appearances on Oprah, or her successful magazine. If you ask someone from Savannah, however, they will tell you that it is her food. In 1999, USA today named Paula Deen's food "International Meal of the Year," but that was merely the start of her meteoric rise to fame and the scores of accolades she's garnered.

Paula started modestly with a catering business called the Bag Lady, working out of her home to make delicious, home-cooked lunches and market them to local businesses. She and her sons built the business, and eventually opened the Lady & Sons downtown in 1989. She has since traveled the world spreading her love for good, old-fashioned Southern cooking. There is hardly a recipe in her restaurant that doesn't include butter or bacon or some other sinful Southern pleasure, but it's the tradition of simple food, shared with friends and family, that keep the lines at this famous restaurant backed up around the block every day of the week. That, plus the chance of seeing Paula Deen!

BELFORD'S
SHRIMP, GREENS, & GRITS

SERVES 4

GRIT CAKES
2 cups water
1 cup Quaker Instant Grits
1 tablespoon chicken base
1 cup flour
1 tablespoon Old Bay Seasoning

COLLARD GREENS
1 (16-ounce) bag cut greens, washed
3 cups water
4 tablespoons butter
1 teaspoon cayenne pepper
1 tablespoon salt

SHRIMP
24 jumbo shrimp, peeled and deveined
4 strips of cooked apple-smoked bacon,
   crumbled
1/2 cup diced scallions
4 tablespoons butter
2 tablespoons vegetable oil
1 cup white wine
1 tomato, finely diced
1/2 cup parmesan cheese

There are few dining spots in Savannah's historic district that wear their history as well as Belford's in City Market. The building's interior decor boasts exposed brick walls, high ceilings, and photographs from bygone eras. Originally built to house Savannah's Hebrew congregation, the building was purchased in 1913 by W.T. Belford for a mere $23,000, and for many years served as the home of Belford's Wholesale Food Company. If you look hard enough, you can still see some of the old company signs painted on the building.

City Market is alive and well today, bustling with both tourists and locals. Because of Chef Kevin McPherson's dedication to good food, Belford's is a cornerstone businesses of the City Market, and this dish has twice been named Southern Living's "Best Entree in Savannah."

The outdoor patio is a great place to enjoy a meal and people watch. Belford's is a successful combination of fine dining and local flavors, which makes it a great place to dine anytime.

In a small stock pot bring 2 cups water to a boil. Add 1 cup Quaker Instant Grits and bring to boil. Reduce heat to medium and continue cooking, stirring the grits until they are creamy. Remove from heat and stir in 1 tablespoon of chicken base. Pour into a shallow baking dish and refrigerate for 2 hours.

Remove Grits from fridge and cut into 8 triangles or squares.

Mix 1 cup flour and 1 tablespoon of Old Bay seasoning and lightly coat the grit cakes. Pan Fry the cakes in hot oil until light golden brown in color, about 3-4 minutes on each side.

To cook the collards, bring water, salt, cayenne pepper, and butter to a boil on high heat in a medium stock pot. Add the greens, reduce heat to medium, and cook for 30 minutes to 1 hour. Greens will be done when they are tender.

To make the shrimp, heat oil in a saute pan over medium-high heat, and saute the bacon for 3 minutes. Add shrimp, white wine and butter, and saute for an additional 3-5 minutes. Salt and pepper to taste.

To serve, arrange 2 grit cakes on a plate with 6 shrimp and collard greens, and top with diced tomatoes, scallions and shredded parmesan cheese.

KASEY'S GOURMET GRILLE
SHRIMP & GRITS

SERVES 6

1/2 red bell pepper, diced
1/2 yellow bell pepper, diced
1/4 of small Vidalia onion, diced
1 leek washed, roots removed (1/2 diced,
    1/2 julienne sliced)
1/2 cup cornstarch
Vegetable oil for frying
15-20 large shrimp
1/2 cup heavy cream
1/4 cup white wine
1 teaspoon Tabasco

3 slices of thick cut smoked bacon,
    cooked and diced
1/4 cup chicken stock
1 tablespoon vegetable oil
1 teaspoon garlic powder

1 (12-ounce) box yellow stone ground grits
1 tablespoon cream cheese, optional

Follow directions on the box to prepare the grits. If cheese is desired, use 1 tablespoon of cream cheese and fold into cooked grits when they are still hot.

In a large saute pan heat vegetable oil over a medium high heat. Add the diced bacon. Once bacon fat starts to render, add shrimp, season with salt and pepper, and saute for 2 minutes. Add peppers, onions, diced leeks, and garlic, and saute for 1 minute. Then add white wine, chicken stock, and Tabasco and cook until the liquid is reduced by half. Add heavy cream, and reduce by half again.

For fried leek garnish, julienne 1/2 leek, dredge in cornstarch and fry in vegetable oil until golden brown.

To plate, place a round of the grits in middle of a large shallow bowl. Arrange the shrimp tails out around the grits. Pour sauce over the top and garnish with fried leeks.

Midtown Savannah has never been known as a dining hotspot, but this neighborhood bistro and wine bar is changing all of that. Located just south of Ardsley Park, this is the upscale dining experience that residents and businesses in the area have needed. Chef and Co-owner Daniel Berman offers a diverse menu that features the finest ingredients—organic produce, fresh seafood, and choice cuts of meat.

Housed in a strip center, the bistro nonetheless achieves the feel of a more upscale dining establishment. During the week, it's a popular lunch spot for a faithful clientele. At night, upscale entrees are served along with great wine pairings. If you need a great place to unwind at the end of a long day, enjoy one of their famous martinis!

Tubby's Tank House
Boiled Shrimp

SERVES 4 TO 6

2 pounds fresh, shell on, domestic, wild
   caught, white shrimp
6 quarts boiling water
Old Bay Seafood Seasoning

Drop the shrimp in boiling water and cook until they float. Remove from the water (they aren't done yet, but they will finish cooking on the way to the table). Sprinkle with seasoning to taste. Serve with cocktail sauce and lemon wedges.

NOTE: If you want to serve cold, chill the shrimp in ice water before seasoning.

Gone fishin, be back at dark-thirty!

- Author Unknown

SCALLOPS

Scallops are the carpetbaggers at Savannah tables. They are not native to Southeastern waters, but we've come to love them so much that you will find a scallop dish on practically any menu in the city. I've included three dishes that are "Savannah-fied" with locally grown tomatoes, Vidalia onions, and sweet fresh corn.

Scallops can be served a number of ways—dressed up enough for a formal dinner (Chatham Club's Scallop Ceviche appetizer), or served as a tasty snack (Sundae Café's Margarita Grilled Scallops). They are perfect little morsels thrown on a grill for a dockside lunch and, to be honest, casual cooking is the heart of Savannah cuisine.

CHEF JOE RANDALL'S
SPRING GREENS AND PAN-SEARED SCALLOPS WITH CITRUS VINAIGRETTE

SERVES 8

4 cups mixed greens
24 large sea scallops, connective muscle removed
1/4 teaspoon salt
1 teaspoon freshly ground black pepper
Flour
2 cups citrus vinaigrette, *see recipe*
2 tablespoons olive oil
2 tablespoons butter
2 cloves fresh garlic, minced

CITRUS VINAIGRETTE
1/4 cup white wine vinegar
1/4 cup fresh lemon juice
1/4 teaspoon lemon zest
1 teaspoon sugar
1 teaspoon salt
1/4 teaspoon freshly ground black pepper
1 1/4 cups peanut oil

"It is my undying devotion to my heritage and the cuisine of the South and my love of sharing it with others that has made me truly joyful."
- Chef Joe Randall

To make the vinaigrette, whisk together the white wine vinegar, lemon juice, lemon zest, sugar, salt and pepper. Continue to whisk while pouring in the peanut oil in a steady stream. Adjust the seasoning to your taste.

To make the scallops, season the scallops with salt and pepper. If you care to use flour, lightly dust the seasoned scallops with flour, and shake off any excess. Heat the olive oil and butter over a medium high heat in a cast iron skillet or saute pan. Add the scallops and garlic and saute for 3 minutes on each side.

To plate the salad, place the mixed greens in the center of each plate, arrange the warm scallops on the greens and top with the citrus vinaigrette. Garnish with chopped chives and serve immediately.

CHATHAM CLUB
SCALLOP CEVICHE

SERVES 8

24 large scallops, cut in half lengthwise
1 1/2 cups champagne vinegar
1 1/2 cups granulated sugar
3 limes, zested
2 limes, juiced
2 tablespoons pink peppercorns, toasted
    and chopped

OVEN ROASTED TOMATOES
12 Roma tomatoes, cut in half lengthwise
1 teaspoon garlic, chopped
1/4 cup balsamic vinegar
1/4 teaspoon salt
1/8 teaspoon ground black pepper
1 tablespoon sugar

2 sprigs fresh basil, chopped
1/4 cup olive oil

AVOCADO MOUSSE
2 avocados, ripe, peeled and seeded
8 medium shallots
1 lime, juiced
2 sprigs basil
1/4 cup heavy cream

GARNISH
1 small red onion, sliced into rings
3 avocados, sliced lengthwise
Frisee, or mixed salad greens
Extra virgin olive oil

Slice the scallops, place in a bowl, cover, and refrigerate.

Mix the champagne vinegar, sugar, lime zest, and lime juice into a small saucepan and bring to a boil to dissolve the sugar. Remove from heat and allow the mixture to cool to room temperature. In a small saute pan, toast pink peppercorns over low heat until you can smell their fragrance. Chop peppercorns and add to vinegar mixture, then pour over the reserved scallops and refrigerate for 2 to 4 hours. These scallops can be refrigerated for up to 6 hours. Remove scallops from the marinade when they are ready to plate.

To prepare the oven roasted tomatoes, halve the tomatoes and place in a bowl. In another bowl, whisk together the garlic, balsamic vinegar, salt, pepper, sugar, chopped basil and olive oil. Pour the mixture over the tomatoes and allow to marinate at least 1 hour. Line a baking pan with a wire rack and set the tomatoes cut side up on the wire rack. Sprinkle any extra marinade lightly over the tomatoes. Bake at 325 degrees F for 1 1/2 hours then place in the refrigerator to cool. When the tomatoes are cool, cut them each in half again. These tomatoes can be made up to 2 days in advance.

To make the avocado mousse, put the basil, shallot, lime juice, and peeled and seeded avocado into a blender. Pulse blender a few times, scraping the sides down after each pulse. Add the heavy cream and blend until the mixture is smooth. This can be prepared up to 2 hours before serving if you place the mousse into a small container and cover with plastic wrap to prevent discoloration.

To serve the dish, place a small amount of avocado mousse near the center of the plate and spread with the back of a spoon. Arrange 6 scallop halves and 6 tomatoes in a circular pattern, alternating the scallops with the tomatoes. Garnish each plate with a little frisee or mixed greens, a few small rounds of red onion, an avocado slice, and a drizzle of extra virgin olive oil.

This prestigious private club is located on the 14th floor of the historic DeSoto Hilton hotel in downtown Savannah. The club, which is named after William Pitt, the Earl of Chatham, opened in 1968 and is known for its elegant dining room overlooking the city, the impeccable service, and an excellent daily menu. The club also features several private rooms, which are available to members for intimate social gatherings and small dinner parties.

The dining room's panoramic view of the nation's largest urban historic district and the majestic Savannah River is part of what inspires great dining at the Chatham Club. The culinary inspirations, however, come from Chef Frederick Nussbaum, who offers elegant Continental cuisine and inventive takes on the region's finest seafood.

SUNDAE CAFÉ
MARGARITA GRILLED SCALLOPS

SERVES 6

MARINADE
1/2 can orange juice concentrate
1 lime, juiced
2 ounces Tequila
1 bunch fresh cilantro, chopped
Pinch of salt and pepper

BLACK BEAN & CORN SALSA
1 (28-ounce) can black beans, drained and rinsed
2 ears fresh corn, cooked and kerneled (may substitute frozen corn, cooked)
1/2 red onion, finely diced
1 bunch fresh cilantro, finely chopped

1 teaspoon cumin
1 jalapeno, diced
1 lime, juiced

RED PEPPER AIOLI
1 (28-ounce) can roasted red peppers, drained and chopped
2 cloves garlic, minced
1 cup mayonnaise

1 pound fresh small scallops (20-30 count)
Corn or flour tortilla chips

Preheat grill to medium high heat.

To make the marinade, combine all ingredients in a bowl, add the scallops, and marinate for 10-15 minutes.

To make the salsa, combine all the ingredients and stir until mixed well.

To make the red pepper aioli, mix the roasted red peppers, garlic, and mayonnaise and chill.

Remove scallops from the marinade and grill them on each side for 2-3 minutes.

Place a layer of chips on the bottom a serving plate. Layer over with the black bean and corn salsa. Add the scallops and spoon on the red pepper Aioli to taste.

Sundae Café brings together the basic elements... in a simple but effective way to deliver a memorable night on Tybee Island.
- Pete Lamb,
Savannah Morning News

INDEX

Aioli, Red Pepper, 92
Ardsley Park, 71, 83
Au Gratin, Shrimp and Crab, 22–23
Avocado Mousse, 91

Bag Lady, 79
Baker, A. J., 24
Balsamic Syrup, 24
Basil Cream Sauce, 79
Bee Road, 23
Belford, W. T., 80
Belford's, 80
Berman, Daniel, 83
Black Bean & Corn Salsa, 92
Blaine, Kirk, 44
Bloody Mary Oyster Shooters, 58–59
Blount, Roy, Jr., 56
Boiled Shrimp, 84–85
Bolitho, Hector, 55
Butter
  Crab, 40
  Sauce, Citrus, 36

Caesar Salad, Fried Oyster, 60–61
Cafe 37, 53, 55
Caper Flowers, Fried, 20
Capt'n Crab's Low Country Boil, 68–69
Caribbean Shrimp, 72–73
Carpenter, Kevin, 24
Carr, Lisa, 18
Carroll, Lewis, 9
Casserole, Seafood, 74–75
Ceviche, Scallop, 90–91
Chatham Club, 91
Cheese Crisps, 60
Cheesecake, Seafood, 24–25
Chef Joe Randall's, 43
Chimney Creek, 68
Chowder, Corn and Crab, 18–19
Chutney, Peach, 32–33
Cilantro Cream Sauce, 39
Citrus
  Butter Sauce, 36
  Vinaigrette, 88
City Market, 80
Clark, Ray, 31
Collard Greens, 80
Columbia Square, 76
Condé Nast Traveler, 49
Confederates on Horseback, 48–49
Connect Savannah, 18, 66, 72
Corn
  Capt'n Crab's Low Country Boil, 68–69
  and Crab Chowder, 18–19
  Salsa, Black Bean &, 92
Cornmeal Fried Oysters, 56–57
Crab(s)
  about, 13

Au Gratin, Shrimp and, 22–23
Butter, 40
Cakes, Savannah, 20–21
Chowder, Corn and, 18–19
Deviled, 16–17
Parmesan Crusted Grouper with Jumbo Lump, 36–37
Seafood Casserole, 74–75
Soup, She, 26–27
Stew, 14–15
Stuffed Flounder, 40–41
Stuffed Shrimp, 78–79
The Crab Shack, 68
Cream Sauces, 23, 39, 56, 79
Crusts, 24, 36
Crystal Beer Parlor, 15

Deen, Bubba, 40
Deen, Paula, 40, 50, 79
DeSoto Hilton, 91
Deviled Crabs, 16–17
Donaldson, Kermit "Red," 23
Dressing
  Caesar, 60
  Oyster, 50–51
Driftaway Cafe, 44

Elsinghorst, Blake, 53

Firefly Cafe, 18
Fish
  about, 29
  Crab Stuffed Flounder, 40–41
  Grouper
    Fingers, Fried, 30–31
    Pan-Roasted Black, 42–43
    Parmesan Crusted, with Jumbo Lump Crabmeat, 36–37
    Sweet Potato-Crusted, 32–33
  Red Snapper
    Pan-Seared, 44–45
    with Roasted Vegetables, Whole, 34–35
  Salmon Cakes with Cilantro Cream Sauce, 38–39
Flanagan, Jack and Belinda, 68
Flay, Bobby, 50
Flounder, Crab Stuffed, 40–41
Food Network, 50, 79
Fried Grouper Fingers, 30–31
Fried Oyster Caesar Salad, 60–61
Fried Oysters, Cornmeal, 56–57
The Frugal Gourmet (Smith), 84

Georgia Shrimp Salad, Watermelon and Wild, 66–67
The Glorious Oyster (Bolitho), 55
Gourmet Magazine, 76
Greens
  Shrimp, Grits &, 80–81

Spring, Pan-Seared Scallops with Citrus Vinaigrette and, 88–89
Grits
  Shrimp, Greens &, 80–81
  Shrimp and, 82–83
Grouper
  Fingers, Fried, 30–31
  Pan-Roasted Black, 42–43
  Parmesan Crusted, with Jumbo Lump Crabmeat, 36–37
  Sweet Potato-Crusted, 32–33

Habersham, James, 26
Habersham Street, 18
Harris, Johnny, 23
Herb River, 36
Historic District, 9–10, 12, 66, 80, 91
Horseradish Sour Cream Sauce, 56

Isle of Hope, 36

James Beard medal, 49
Jepson Center For The Arts, 20
Johnny Harris Restaurant, 23

Kasey's Gourmet Grille, 83
Kayak Kafé, 66
Kenny, Michael, 58

The Lady & Sons, 40, 79
Larson, Doug, 32
Lazaretto Creek, 10, 65

Margarita Grilled Scallops, 92–93
Marinade, Margarita, 92
Mason, Susan, 71
McPherson, Kevin, 80
Midtown, 16, 83
Mousse, Avocado, 91
Mrs. Wilkes' Boardinghouse Restaurant, 49, 75

Nesbit, Martha Giddens, 50, 62
Nichols, John and Phillip, 15
North Beach Grill, 72
Nussbaum, Frederick, 91

O'Connor, Liam and Darcy, 18
Olde Pink House, 26, 60
Olympia Café, 35
Oprah, 79
Owens-Thomas House, 20
Oyster(s)
  about, 47
  Confederates on Horseback, 48–49
  Dressing, 50–51
  Fried, Caesar Salad, 60–61
  Fried, Cornmeal, 56–57
  Po' Boy, 54-55

Roast, Winter, 47
Scalloped, 62–63
Shooters, Bloody Mary, 58–59
Stew, 52-53

Pan-Roasted Black Grouper, 42–43
Pan-Seared
  Red Snapper, 44–45
  Scallops with Citrus Vinaigrette, Spring Greens and, 88–89
Pappas, Nick, 35
Parks, Jamie, 20
Parmesan
  Cheese Crisps, 60
  Crusted Grouper with Jumbo Lump Crabmeat, 36–37
Peach Chutney, Sweet Potato-Crusted Grouper with, 32–33
Pearl's Saltwater Grill, 36, 56
Pesto, 44, 79
Pickled Shrimp, 70–71
The Pink House, 26, 60
Pitt, William, 91
The Planter's Tavern, 26
Po' Boy, Oyster, 54–55
Polk's Fresh Market, 66
Potatoes, Roasted, 35
Powers, Anna, 76
Provencal Tomatoes, 44

Quattlebaum, Robyn and Michelle, 44
Quiche, Shrimp and Onion, 76–77

Randall, Joe, 29, 43
Red Pepper Aioli, 92
Red Snapper
  Pan-Seared, 44–45
  with Roasted Vegetables, Whole, 34–35
Remoulade Sauce, 20, 53
Retsas, Bonnie, 39
Rice, Savannah Red, 43
River Street, 31, 35
Roasting
  Black Grouper, Pan-, 42–43
  Oyster, 47
  Potatoes, 35
  Tomatoes, Oven-, 91
  Vegetables, 35
Roux, 79
Russo, Charles, Jr., 16, 29
Russo's Seafood, 16, 29

Salad
  Caesar, Fried Oyster, 60–61
  Watermelon and Wild Georgia Shrimp, 66–67
Salmon Cakes with Cilantro Cream Sauce, 38–39
Salsa, Black Bean & Corn, 92
Sandfly, 44

Sandwiches, Oyster Po' Boy, 54-55
Sauce
  Basil Cream, 79
  Cilantro Cream, 39
  Citrus Butter, 36
  Cream, 23
  Horseradish Sour Cream, 56
  Pesto, 44, 79
  Red Pepper Aioli, 92
  Remoulade, 20, 53
  Roux, 79
Savannah
  historic district, 9–10, 12, 66, 80, 91
  history of, 9–10
  midtown, 16, 83
  riverside, 31, 35
Savannah Crab Cakes, 20–21
Savannah International Trade and Convention Center, 20
Savannah Magazine, 40, 50
Savannah Red Rice, 43
Savannah River, 9
Savor... Savannah, 20, 58
Scalloped Oysters, 62–63
Scallops
  about, 87
  Ceviche, 90–91
  Margarita Grilled, 92–93
  Pan-Seared, with Citrus Vinaigrette, Spring Greens, 88–89
Seafood
  Casserole, 74–75
  Cheesecake, 24–25
Seaside Sisters, 10
17Hundred90, 76
She Crab Soup, 26–27
Shrimp
  about, 65
  Au Gratin, Crab and, 22–23
  Boiled, 84–85
  Capt'n Crab's Low Country Boil, 68–69
  Caribbean, 72–73
  Crab-Stuffed, 78–79
  Greens & Grits, 80–81
  and Grits, 82–83
  Pickled, 70–71
  Quiche, Onion and, 76–77
  Salad, Watermelon and Wild Georgia, 66–67
  Seafood Casserole, 74–75
Smith, Jeff, 84
Snapper. See Red Snapper
Soho South Café, 39
Soup, She Crab, 26–27. See also Stew
Sour Cream Sauce, Horseradish, 56
Southern Living, 80
Spriggs, George, 72
Stew
  Crab, 14–15

Oyster, 52-53
Stinogel, Sharon, 18
Strickland, Sam, 31
Sundae Café, 24, 29, 32
Susan Mason Catering, 71
Susan Mason's Silver Service (Mason), 71
Sweet Potato-Crusted Grouper with Peach Chutney, 32–33
Swift, Jonathan, 47

37th Street, 53
Thunderbolt marina, 31
Tomatoes
  Oven-Roasted, 91
  Provencal, 44
Troupe Square, 18
Tubby's Tank House, 31, 84
Turner's Creek, 40
Tybee Island, 10, 24, 65, 72
Tybrisa Pier, 65

Uncle Bubba's Oyster House, 40
USA Today, 79

Varlagas, Vasilis, 35
Vegetables. See also Tomatoes
  Roasted, Whole Red Snapper with, 34–35
  Shrimp, Greens & Grits, 80–81
Victory Drive, 23
Vinaigrette, Citrus, 88

Warren Square, 26
Watermelon and Wild Georgia Shrimp Salad, 66–67
Weikart, David, 36
Whitemarsh Island, 40
Whole Red Snapper with Roasted Vegetables, 34–35
Wilkes, Mrs., 49
Williams, Ansley, 31
Williams, Patrick, 31
Winter Oyster Roast, 47